Samsung Galaxy S10 & S10 plus:

User's Guide: 100+1 Tips and Tricks to Master Your Samsung S10, S10 plus & 10e

ISBN:9781096847885

CONTENTS

Thank you for purchasing this book!

We always try to give more value then you expect. That's why we've updated the content and you can get it for FREE. You can get the digital version for free because you bought the print version.

The book is under the match program from Amazon. You can find how to do this using next URL: https://www.amazon.com/gp/digital/ep-landing-page

I hope it will be useful for you.

Introduction

The Samsung Group is one of the largest conglomerates in the business world, in its homeland, South Korea.

The Samsung Group was founded in Daegu, Korea, on March 1, 1938. Its founder, entrepreneur Byung-Chull Lee (1910-1987), whose starting capital was only 30,000 won ($ 2,000), called Samsung (Samsung Trading Co), translated from Korean, "three stars ". On the first logos of the company, these three stars are present in different variations. One of the most plausible versions of the origin of the name says that the entrepreneur had three sons. This version is also supported by the fact that the company, in the spirit of many Asian firms, remained a family business, transferring and multiplying capital among relatives (and making a relative of the one who managed to enter the business stand out. Inter-clan marriages are one of the business traditions in Asia). The entrepreneur, who according to some sources never received a degree, became one of the most famous and most respected people in Korea, the Korean equivalent of the Nobel Prize. The Ho-Am Prize, founded by Samsung and awarded for outstanding achievements in science and technology, was named after him.

A decade after the launch of the first smartphone of the Galaxy S line, Samsung Electronics presents a series of new flagship devices, Galaxy S10, and lays the foundation for the next decade of mobile innovations. Amongst the premium new products, the main model of the Galaxy S10 is a larger model of the Galaxy S10+, including a ceramic version with 1TB of internal memory and a Galaxy S10e in a compact flat-screen case. Innovations bring impressions from using the phone to a new level thanks to innovations in the most relevant areas for users: display, camera, and performance

Chapter 1 What you need to know about the Samsung Galaxy S10 and S10e before you buy it.

In 2019, customers were waiting for new solutions from Samsung designers. Galaxy S9 was the same as Galaxy S8, with minor improvements to the exterior. It's time to surprise. And the company took drastic measures, releasing completely frameless phones. They followed the mainstream in the smartphone industry and generated devices with a fresh, exceptional design while retaining the main features of the line, such as the rounded edges of the screen.

Galaxy S10 and S10+ are interesting primarily in the way of

unlocking. The ultrasonic sub-screen scanner detects the imprint of even a wet, sticky, or dirty finger, which optical sensors are not capable of. At Vivo NEX, we had problems with it. This was not the case here. The finger can be applied more carelessly and at any angle. The sensor will determine the owner without any problems.

This method of unlocking appeared on smartphones in the summer of 2018. Samsung was not the first, but it made the most practical sensor. And this is the whole essence of the new Galaxy. They are not the first to seek a solution. Sub-screen fingerprint scanners, triple cameras, reverse charging and "holey" displays can be found in other smartphones. The phones take all the trend capabilities and make them better.

There is also a face scanner. Not a new solution, but it will please those who have crossed a few generations. This is a 2D scanner, less reliable and less accurate. Bloggers have noticed that it can be fooled by a photo. There is a video on the web when the phone is unlocked from the picture. We did not find this and no complaints arose.

Popularity in social networks has arisen thanks to the "leaky" screens. There are a lot of wallpapers on the Internet, where the cutout will look like an element of the picture. There is also an application with them on Google Play, and in the future, they will be collected in the "Wallpapers and Themes" section. The "leaky" screen means making the frames as thin as possible. It does not offer other advantages: the video is played in 16: 9 proportions, there are black bars around the edges, and game developers stretch the picture only when the camera does not close an important interface element. So, PUBG does not play on the full screen with a black stripe near the selfie camera but does so on Assassin's Creed Rebellion and Asphalt 9.

In terms of other characteristics, the Galaxy S10 does not suit the revolution, but it certainly does not disappoint. The smartphone does not strive to be the best at one thing, like Huawei's flagship camera, but offers a set of optimal features. Screen – just from this series. The display did not break the record for brightness or other parameters. It is simply very high quality. Wide viewing angle – you can tilt back and the image will not lose contrast. Very rich colors – if you turn on the dark theme, the display will merge with the frames. High brightness – it is convenient to use a clear day.

The most inconvenient thing about this smartphone is the display. This edge is a big minus of this phone. They are less curved than the Galaxy S9, but they still interfere with typing. If you reach the opposite edge with your finger, you can accidentally click on another letter. There are inconveniences when scrolling social networks. Random clicks on pages are possible. In general, the curved edges highlight Samsung's flagships and make them more aesthetic, but in fact, this element is impractical.

The second nice feature is sound. The smartphone is very loud. With it you will definitely not sleep through the alarm by setting the volume to maximum. On the device, it is pleasant to watch videos without headphones, and if you wish, you can activate Dolby Atmos technology in the notification blind, the sound will become even louder and more spacious. With this performance, the device can even replace a portable speaker.

The smartphone runs on Android 9 with One UI, a new, redesigned Samsung shell. And most of the pleasant sensations were obtained precisely because of this. The main innovations are gesture control and a dark theme, and the strongest side is smoothness, atypical for Android. Externally, the firmware is similar to iOS: icons of the same form, the same animations of pressing keys, opening applications and exiting the multitasking menu. And this is the main advantage: it is comfortable to type text on a smartphone, from short notes and messages in instant messengers to long articles like this. No need to change the animation in the settings and install third-party keyboards. Everything is so convenient.

When you become acquainted with the phone, it is advisable to immediately explore the settings, where you can find a lot of great features. For example, in the notification curtain, turn on the "Edge Backlight", from which the edges of the screen will light up when receiving notifications. I was disappointed only by the lock screen; notifications are not shown in the usual way, but in the form of pictograms. You can view them by clicking on the icons, then the notification curtain will open. Some users like it, others it infuriates. It would be more logical to provide an option to the user for exactly how he wants to see notifications.

The camera is the moment when the manufacturer followed the trend and partially neglected modern solutions. There are three modules, as in most of the flagships of 2019: a wide, ultra-wide, and telephoto lens. You can switch them by clicking on the icons on top of the shutter button. All three sensors produce images with good detail saturated colors. Sometimes it brings a white balance, and in this case, photo editors like VSCO and Adobe Lightroom come to the rescue.

The camera does not have a night mode, although almost all Android vendors added it last year. The manufacturer believes that the algorithms will cope in the normal shooting mode. And they cope. Photo quality is above average. The detailing is at a good level, but a lot of noise appears in the frame. They are unevenly diverging in the picture: in lighter areas there are more of them; in darker area, on the contrary, a less pleasant effect is obtained.

The strength of this smartphone is video quality. The detailing is good, as are the sound and stabilization. For clarity, we compared the Galaxy S10 with the iPhone 7. In the test both smartphones behaved with dignity. The flagship of this year was naturally better, but not much. The main drawback of the Apple smartphone is the frequent picture tweaks. Samsung also has them, but they are much smaller. Video stabilization, in our opinion, is of equal quality. Samsung also has colder colors, good or not. A matter of taste.

And the front camera does not ass any minuses or to pluses of the smartphone. There are modes for single and group self, despite the presence of a single sensor. They switch the same way as the lenses of the main camera: the corresponding icons are located above the shutter button. In ideal conditions, decent photos are obtained, but in low light conditions the detail is greatly reduced, and in a closed room or in artificial light the white balance is very noticeable and the colors become unnatural.

The performance is something that cannot be doubted in any device released by this company: all games run at maximum graphics settings. In the process, the smartphone heats up, but no stronger than its competitors. Autonomy is average. With moderate use at the end of the day, 10–15% of the charge remains. With active multimedia playback and using it in modem mode, the battery is discharged by late evening, so it would be good to buy a power bank. Also, there is reverse wireless charging, designed primarily for accessories with a small amount of battery. We failed to test the function on them, and the S10E charge from S10 proved that, in this case, the function is completely meaningless. Within an hour the smartphone was charged by 20%, but at the same time the S10 was discharged by 50%.

Samsung was able to make a balanced flagship with an attractive design, almost without drawbacks, although without exceptional features. It fits almost any user requests. There can be many parameters in priority: the screen, the sound, the smooth shell, the main camera, the modern ways of unlocking, and in each case the Galaxy S10 is a worthy option. This should be the second smartphone of the flagship series with slightly reduced functionality. Although it does not possess enough exceptional features like a double selfie camera with depth of field control, as in the S10 +, or an enlarged optical zoom, to undoubtedly be a premium smartphone.

The phone should offer the main features of premium models and cost far less, so some components in it will be cheaper. Koreans went a different way: a smartphone with a cheap LCD-screen and one camera receiving the Face ID feature and Depth Control function, which controls the degree of background blur. Galaxy S10e was deprived of the main chip in the S10 and S10+. There is no sub-screen fingerprint scanner, but all other interesting features remain at the premium level.

Instead of a sub-screen sensor, this smartphone has an external one. It is located on the right side and is combined with the power button. When using it, there are no problems. Due to the miniature body, it is easy to reach the right-hand side with your thumb and the left-hand side with your index finger for the scanner. The phone is slightly larger than the iPhone 7, so the second hand is not involved.

But in the Galaxy S10e there is an AMOLED-screen, not an LCD, as in the iPhone XR. The resolution is Full HD +, not Quad HD +, but the brightness and color palette are at the same flagship level. There are no issues watching video comfortably from any angle, when using a clear day. At maximum brightness you will always get a clear image.

The display here, in contrast to the S10, is flat, and in some cases compared to other, more premium models, this turns out to be a plus. On smartphones with curved edges, it is felt that the content is closer, but scrolling social networks and typing text is not convenient for everyone – random clicks often occur. Flat edges and slightly thickened frames look less impressive, but there are no problems with random clicks. Interestingly, even with flat edges on the smartphone, there is an "Edge backlight", when the edges light up when receiving notifications, and the Apps Edge additional menu where you can put the most important applications.

The smartphone also retains the reverse charge, so you can feed the wireless headphones and smartwatches from the case. Apparently, the company decided to promote accessories in this way, and not by abandoning the connectors.

The dual camera includes a wide module and a telephoto lens. It is devoid of zoom. The increase in frame quality is lost, but otherwise, the camera is the flagship and one of the best on the market. The sensors in it are the same as in S10 and S10+. With them you get decent photos in almost any condition without having to modify the settings. It is especially good at separating the object in the foreground from the background, which turns out as an imitation of the bokeh effect.

The speakers are the same as in the S10. Very loud, and when you turn on the Dolby Atmos technology, it becomes even louder and more spacious. The performance is the same: the battery lasts a day to work with active use - social networks, instant messengers, and even YouTube in windowed mode when a lot of energy is consumed. At night, you must put the smartphone on a charge.

With such a set of features, the "cheaper" Galaxy S10e is a fully-fledged flagship with a trendy appearance and top features. If you select it instead of S10 and S10+, you will lose only the optical zoom and the sub-screen fingerprint scanner. For all other parameters it works at the same top level. And unlike the S8 and S9, the device offers a more modern, completely frameless case.

Whether such a model will be successful in the Android segment is unknown. If the frameless iPhone with Face ID popularity was guaranteed, then in the case of the S10e everything is foggy. The start of sales also does not inspire optimism, the model is considered the worst of all the new products. Nevertheless, Samsung managed to generate a top-end device, painlessly reducing its cost.

The alignment is this: if there is no opportunity or desire to buy S10 and S10+, but you want a Samsung, the most rational choice is S10e, and not its cheaper predecessor.

Samsung Galaxy S10, Galaxy S10, and Galaxy S10e are recognized as the best smartphones in the framework of a study conducted by the International Consumer Research Association International Consumer Research & Testing. New items took the first, second, and third positions in the ranking. Where last year's flagship Samsung Galaxy Note9 was leading, it is now in fourth place.

Smartphones S10 and S10+ are very durable: as a result of the drum test, they got off with only small scratches. In addition, the S10 phones received very high scores for communication quality and processor speed. The quality of the camera has improved, too. For example, for the resolution of the front-facing camera, these smartphones received the highest points the study notes.

To date, Samsung smartphones occupy 7 of the top 10 positions in the ranking. The top 10 also includes the Galaxy S9, Galaxy S9, and Galaxy S8, located in seventh, eighth and ninth places, respectively.

Chapter 2. Design

In the global sense, there have been no major changes. It is still a glass smartphone with an aluminum frame and panels bent to the corners. Of the noticeable changes, besides the cut-out in the screen, the shape of the block of cameras has changed, where they added another sensor. But in general, the device does not look like something new, especially if the user is previously familiar with previous models.

The size of the case has become quite a bit larger, but also thinner: 149.9 × 70.4 × 7.8mm, weight - 157 grams. All because of the increased screen. But it doesn't really affect usability. For such a large display, it is quite a small case. It is convenient to hold a smartphone in your hand and then toss it into a pocket where it doesn't bother you too much.

The main controls remained in place. You can now reassign the Bixby call key with native tools. Previously, you had to resort to third-party software, but the next update will fix this issue. But most of all I like the fact that the S10 remains one of the few flagships that do not get rid of the classic headphone jack. The standard of protection against moisture and dust also does not change standard: IP68.

Despite the slight changes in design, there is no feeling of novelty from the device. But the smartphone looks great. As far as can be judged from the test copy, it will be very difficult to find serious flaws in the assembly. But for those who waited for some significant design updates, this model will not please you.

Display

In S10, the screen is called Infinity O-Display. Now its diagonal is 6.1 inches (in the previous model it was 5.8"). For lovers of thin frames, there is just sight from all sides. Curled sides have not gone anywhere. They look beautiful, but in some positions can you accidentally touch something, and the system does not always recognize it by a random touch. You can get used to it. Your hands will adapt themselves to avoid such clicks in future.

The resolution has grown a bit and is now equal to 3040×1440 pixels, which in turn amounts to 550 PPI (20 less than the previous model). The aspect ratio of 19:9, as usual, will force you to choose when viewing a standard video between the black frames on the sides or a slightly cropped picture at the top and bottom. In the second case, you still need to put up with the cut-out of the camera in the corner. Rarely in this place are important pictures of the data, but if it is a gameplay video, then some element of HUD

16

may still be there. But more and more often you will come across suitable "wide" content. But the adaptation of some applications to the cut-out will have to wait (for example, I got a mismatch in Android Auto).

The picture quality, as always with Samsung, is excellent. The Super AMOLED matrix evolved into Dynamic AMOLED and received support for HDR10 +. The screen has two main modes: Vivid and Natural. The first one, as usual, is oversaturated, bright, and colorful, but it allows you to slightly adjust the color temperature to suit personal preferences. Natural just falls under the DCI-P3 color profile, but when switching it looks dim against the background of the standard one. Regardless of the selected profile, the screen looks gorgeous and absolutely nothing to complain about.

Backlit, everything is in order. Our measurements showed a maximum of 430 cd / m² indoors, but under direct sunlight, this figure is much higher (the display itself adjusts the brightness limit depending on the situation). Indeed, on a sunny day, it is practically not necessary to cover the display with your hand. Otherwise, the screen works as usual. The sensor works perfectly, there is Always-On-Display, blue filter for the evening, and so on.

Chapter 3 Getting started with your new phone

The first thing you need to do after buying a smartphone is to give it a basic setting. This includes choosing a language, enabling data transfer, entering data from a Google account, etc. In some cases, the system may also ask you to enter data from other accounts. Let's look at the initial setup process in more detail:

Your phone's settings are no different from Android device settings.

Setting up most Android smartphones begins with the choice of language. You will be presented with a list of languages supported by this version of the operating system, from which you need to choose the one that suits you. After selecting it, click "Next", which in our case looks like an arrow.

Then, you will need to connect to the Internet. That is, you need to connect to a Wi-Fi network. Choose a network that is home to you. You can skip this step by clicking "Next", however, it is recommended to do this only if a SIM card with a connected mobile Internet is inserted into the smartphone.

Then enter the password for your home Wi-Fi network and click "Connect".

It is possible that the connection test will start. It is also possible that the smartphone will provide an opportunity to update the firmware. The system may also offer to transfer data from another device running Android. If you do not need it, click "Skip".

Full use of the smartphone is impossible without creating a Google account. If you already had an Android smartphone, just enter your account details. If you do not have such an account yet, then click on "Create a new account". Skipping this step is not recommended, because you will not be able to access the Google Play app store and many other features.

Next, you need to enter your Gmail email address, click "Next", then all you have to do is enter your password, then press the above button.

The system will offer you the option to download the applications that were installed on your previous smartphone. To do this, select the brand of the device you used, tick the programs you need (you can leave a tick next to "All applications") and click "Next".

The system will prompt you to activate Google services. It is recommended to leave a tick next to all items and click "Next."

Further, the system can introduce you to the main elements of the interface. Just press the "OK".

Wait for the download and installation of all the applications that were used on your last smartphone. This can be a very lengthy process.

At this, primary settings can be considered complete. It should be noted that depending on the device manufacturer, the actions you take may vary. Just follow the directions on the smartphone screen and you cannot go wrong.

If you want to achieve maximum comfort, it is better to continue the settings.

In addition to all of the above, you must configure email. The email address of Gmail will already be hammered into the parameters of the corresponding application. But you may have other email addresses that you want to add to the Gmail application.

Some useful recommendations

After you have completed all the settings, we recommend that you turn on power saving mode, which will save battery power. Go to: Settings - My device. And turn on energy saving (check all necessary checkboxes). For the same purpose, we recommend that you turn on and off, as soon as it is not necessary, such options as GPS, Bluetooth or NFC, etc. Do not forget that all sorts of animations, vibrating alert, etc. are also enemies of energy saving. If you plan to make purchases through Google Play, we recommend binding your card.

- Take care of installing antivirus for Android

- To complete the battery, try to follow simple rules of use

- Try not to keep your smartphone in the cold

- Try to prevent the battery from completely discharging

- Charge the battery completely. This will increase the recharge cycle of the smartphone

Chapter 4 How to use Fingerprint Scanner

The smartphone is able to recognize the owner through a scan of the face. To do this, use the front camera. The method is not new and is actively used even in budget models. Its disadvantage is reliability, because, with the help of a banal video with the face of the owner, you can "open" the protection (the manufacturer warns about this when setting up). In general, it works, but I tried to pay more attention to the new fingerprint scanner.

A notable distinguishing feature of the S10 is the fingerprint sensor, which is built into the screen. It is ultrasonic and, unlike optical, it can work better in difficult conditions when the fingers are wet or there is a lot of light around. The sensor is located at the bottom of the screen, in the area of the first row of desktop icons.

On a locked display, the system highlights its location with the corresponding icon. Getting used to the position is not difficult at all. It is another thing if you do not get it right away, you will have to make another attempt, and the sensor is not tactilely felt. But in the case of "direct hit", it works quickly and most often accurately.

Chapter 5 The hardware

The model is built on Android 9 with One UI. The software is perfectly implemented in it. It is comfortable and beautiful. This version of One UI 1.1 is slightly different compared to the one that is available on previous flagships since mid-January 2019.

Of the new features, I note Bixby Routines; these are templates with different actions that the user can customize. It is very convenient, and was met in the form of third-party automation programs on the market, but it is good that it is part of the system. You can customize many actions; however, see for yourself in the screenshots.

In the usual menu, Samsung removed many applications. For

example, there is no Play Music and various other icons. Everything fits compactly and, as a result, many useful applications need to be downloaded.

In terms of multimedia, there are no new discoveries here, AKG headphones are excellent, and there is Dolby Atmos. It works well in games. The sound component of the device is good. I will not dwell on this in detail, otherwise the review threatens to become dimensionless.

Samsung One UI

Samsung One UI is a new look at smartphone management. The Samsung TouchWiz user interface, which the company introduced along with its Galaxy S smartphones, was strongly criticized for several reasons. In 2016, Samsung debuted with the Samsung Experience UI shell as part of the Android Nougat update for the Galaxy S7. Since then, Experience UI has been the main interface for the Korean company's smartphones and tablets. When the form factor of the smartphone has changed, and large displays have become commonplace, the need has arisen for an updated interface. The company was fully aware of this problem and developed a new interface - Samsung One UI, whose main task is to maximally simplify working with large screens, as well as to improve gesture support. This is the entire interface of the Samsung One UI.

The new interface was first mentioned at a developer conference in San Francisco, during which the Korean company shared its vision of the future of smartphones with guests, showing a few pictures and explaining why such changes were needed. Representatives of the company have repeatedly said that the new graphical shell is designed not only for our usual smartphones and tablets but will also work on models with a flexible screen with a large diagonal in the opened state. The name One UI itself hints at the opportunity to work with one hand. Looking ahead, I can say that Samsung still managed to create a user-friendly interface that allows you to control your smartphone with one hand. It is based on the new version of Android 9 Pie.

Night mode

They talked about it a lot and for a long time, arguing, cursing, calling, and finally, it appeared. Night mode. Yes, in the new Samsung One UI interface it is now quite easy to enable a dark theme. The most interesting thing is that it is system-wide, that is, it works not only in one kind of application but throughout the system. If you want to use the night mode, then you have to activate it. To do this, open "Settings", go to the "Screen" section, where you just turn on "Night mode". It makes the background in most Samsung applications completely black, which not only pleases the eye but also helps to extend battery life.

Samsung smartphones use AMOLED displays. Here, black becomes really black, without any impurities and shades. It is also possible to configure the night mode to automatically turn on at night.

Samsung One UI makes access to the big screen easier

It is impossible not to talk about the fundamental changes in the quick setup panel. Since the Samsung One UI is based on Android 9 Pie, the blue connection buttons are now displayed. To be honest, it is very similar to the solution on iOS.

As already mentioned, One UI is designed to simplify the use of a large device with one hand and the transfer of the content that you use within reach. The idea is quite simple and has the right to life and, perhaps, imitation. Look at the upper half and interact with the lower. This new design can be seen in all Samsung applications and even on the quick settings panel. Swipe your finger twice on the panel, and all the quick setup will go down to the bottom half of the display.

For example, in that moment, when you open the "Settings" menu, you will notice that the upper half is empty. The word "Settings" is written in the center, in a rather large font. Of course, someone will say that a lot of empty, unused space remains, but believe me, this is really practical and convenient. In fact, this innovation makes the interface look cleaner and less cluttered. At the bottom are the real, necessary parameters, so that you can easily access them without using both hands.

The same design can be found in the gallery, messages, alarm clock, calendar, Bixby, and in almost all Samsung applications. This is useful on such a large and cumbersome phone as Galaxy Note9 or Samsung Galaxy S10 & S10+. And, given that when you remove the front panels, the screen size has increased, it is expected that future Samsung smartphones will only become larger, and the Samsung One UI user interface ensures that you can interact with them.

It is worth paying attention to the notifications, which are now transformed and look fresh, beautiful, and unusually stylish. The developers have tried to maximize the perception of the new interface. Some applications are now able to work in the dark, and each is distinguished by its color and location.

I had to use both hands, for example, when opening a folder, launchpad, or dragging the quick settings panel. In fact, even this is not a problem if you have one-handed operation enabled. It minimizes the entire user interface to about one-third the size by swiping diagonally up from the bottom right or bottom left corner of the screen.

One could say a few words about Bixby widgets. You can easily jump into them if you move from the main screen to the left, but few use them. Although there you can find a lot of interesting things. Maybe you should go there at least to look. What if you like it?

Support navigation gestures

The Samsung One User Interface UI also introduces a new gesture-based navigation feature. This is a proprietary version of Samsung and not the one that comes with an Android Pie, for example, on Google Pixel or Huawei smartphones. To be honest, I'm not a big fan of gestures based on Android 9 Pie. I prefer the navigation buttons, especially since there is plenty of room for them in the Samsung Galaxy S10 & S10+. If we talk about the gestures of Samsung, they are simple and understandable, to a large extent. This is a key feature of One UI. But still, you will need time to get used to them.

Pressing the navigation buttons is replaced with vertical scrolling from the bottom up of the display. And gestures work quite simply.

Swipe up from the bottom middle to go to the home screen, swipe up from the bottom right to go back, and swipe up from the bottom left to open the multitasking window. The multitasking screen shows the latest applications located horizontally, frequently used applications at the bottom, and the search bar at the top.

I want to talk a little about one important change. Samsung

smartphones have a very convenient split-screen mode. This makes it possible to run two applications at once. But often users do not know how to use it. In the new user interface, it can be enabled in multitasking mode. It's simple. In multitasking mode, each application has its own icon at the top, which you should click on. There you will be able to run in split-screen mode or open in pop-up window mode. The screen is divided in half and you can open the second application to use them simultaneously.

In general, the new Samsung One UI interface pleasantly surprises. There are also great design elements. This makes your Samsung Galaxy S10 & S10+ more fashionable. The new graphical shell Samsung One UI is thus a kind of bridge from conventional smartphones to bending.

Chapter 6 Transferring Data from an Existing Phone to the Galaxy S 10

If you had a lot of important information on your old phone, then when buying a new one, you will want to transfer such data to your new phone. In this chapter, we will look at how to do it.

Methods of Data transfer on Samsung Galaxy S 10

There are several ways to transfer information from one Samsung device to another – the use of proprietary utility Smart Switch, synchronization with a Samsung or Google account, the use of third-party programs. Consider each one of them.

Smart switch

Samsung has developed a proprietary application for transferring data from one device (not just Galaxy) to other smartphones of its own production. The application is called Smart Switch and exists in the format of a mobile utility or software for desktop computers running Windows and Mac OS.

Smart Switch allows you to transfer data via USB-cable or via Wi-Fi. In addition, you can use the desktop version of the application and transfer information between smartphones using a computer. The algorithm for all methods is similar, so consider the transfer using the example of a wireless connection through a phone application.

In addition to the Play Market, this application is in the Galaxy Apps store.

You should install Smart Switch on both devices. Then you run the application on the old device. Select the "Wi-Fi" transmission method ("Wireless"). Then you should choose a wireless connection in Smart Switch Mobile.

Note: On Galaxy S8 / S8 + and above devices, the Smart Switch is integrated into the system and is located in the address "Settings" - "Cloud and accounts" - "Smart Switch".

Then you should select "Send.". Further, you should choose to send data from the old device to Smart Switch Mobile. Then you go to the new device. Open Smart Switch and select "Receive". Then you choose to receive data on a new device in Smart Switch Mobile. In the OS selection window of the old device, check the item "Android". You should select the type of device to connect to Smart Switch Mobile and on the old device you click on "Connect". If everything is correct you connect old and new devices in Smart Switch Mobile.

You will be prompted to select categories of data that will be transferred to the new device. Together with them, the application will display the time required for the transfer.

You should select data categories from your old device in Smart Switch Mobile. Then mark the necessary information and click "Send". Then on the new device, you confirm receipt of the files.

Choose to receive data from an old device on a new one in Smart Switch Mobile

After the indicated time has passed, Smart Switch Mobile will report a successful transfer.

Finish working with the Smart Switch Mobile on the new device. You should click "Close app".

This method is extremely simple but using the Smart Switch you cannot transfer data and settings of third-party applications, as well as the cache and saved games.

Synchronization with Samsung and Google accounts

The simplest possible way to transfer data from one Samsung device to another is to use the built-in Android data synchronization tool through Google and Samsung service accounts. This is done like this:

On the old device, you need to go to "Settings" - "General" and select "Backup and reset". Then you choose in the settings Backup and reset to transfer data from Samsung to Samsung. There you will find "Archive data". You need to select archiving to transfer data from Samsung to Samsung. Then you go back to the previous window and tap on "Accounts". Next, you need to go to the accounts to transfer data from Samsung to Samsung. Then select "Samsung account". Select a Samsung account to transfer data from Samsung to Samsung. Then tap on "Sync All." After that click Sync Samsung account to transfer data from Samsung to Samsung

Wait until the information is copied to the Samsung cloud storage.

On a new smartphone, log in to the same account in which you backed up the data. By default, the automatic synchronization feature is active on Android, so after a while, the data will appear on your device.

For a Google account, the actions are almost identical, only you need to select "Google". You need to select a Google account to transfer data from Samsung to Samsung

This method, despite its simplicity, is also limited. It is impossible to transfer music and applications that are not installed via the Play Market or Galaxy Apps in this way.

Google photo

If you need to transfer only your photos, then Google Photo can perfectly cope with this task. Using it is quite simple. You need to download Google Photo

Install the app on both Samsung devices. Go into it first on the old one. You need to swipe your finger to the right to access the main menu. Then enter the Google Photo settings to sync pictures on Samsung devices. Next, select "Settings." Then in the settings, click on the item "Start and sync."

Sign in to Startup Google Photos to sync pictures on Samsung devices

Entering this menu item, you activate synchronization by clicking on the switch.

Enable photo sync in Google Photos for transfer between Samsung devices

If you use multiple Google accounts, select the one you want.

On the new device, log in to the account where you turned on synchronization, and repeat steps 1-4. After some time, photos from a previous Samsung smartphone will be available on the smartphone being used now.

Chapter 7 Tips and tricks for your Galaxy S10

Many owners of these cool phones are not aware of the cool things their phone can do. In this chapter, we will describe them in detail.

Bixby button

The company finally decided on changes in the operation of the call button of the voice assistant Bixby. Now it can be reassigned to any other action.

For example, if you assign Instagram, Google, Spotify, or another application to this button, one click will be required to open it. Double-clicking will launch Bixby, as well as pressing withhold.

Smart Wi-Fi

Representatives of the Galaxy S10 series received support for proprietary technology for Wi-Fi, which provides the uninterrupted connection to the network by seamlessly switching between Wi-Fi and LTE. Everything happens automatically and invisibly to the user.

In addition, the Galaxy S10 received support for the Wi-Fi 6 standard: it provides increased Wi-Fi connection speed when connected to a compatible router.

Triple Camera

The Galaxy S10 and S10+ were the first Samsung flagship devices with a triple camera module. And this is not a banal jumble of sensors for the sake of quantity but is a must-have solution, both for portrait shooting and for panoramic photos with extreme viewing angles.

Both smartphones use the main camera with dual optical image stabilization. It consists of a 12-megapixel telephoto sensor with an f / 2.4 aperture, a 12-megapixel wide-angle with an aperture switchable between f / 1.5 and f / 2.4, and a 16-megapixel ultra-wide angle (f / 2.2). Video stabilization software. There is autofocus on Dual Pixel technology, digital zoom with zooming up to 10X, and advanced HRD mode.

How to do factory reset on your Samsung

This seemingly difficult task can be solved in several ways. Consider each of them in order of complexity of execution and potential problems.

Warning: resetting the settings will erase all user data on your device! We strongly recommend making a backup before starting.

Method 1: System Tools

The Samsung company has provided users with the option of hard reset of the device through the device settings.

Enter the "Settings" in any way possible.

In the "General Settings" group there is the "Backup and Reset" item. Enter this item with a single tap.

The settings menu in Samsung smartphone. Find the option "Reset data". Its location depends on the version of Android and firmware of the device. Reset data in the settings of the Samsung smartphone

The application will warn you about the removal of all stored user information (including user accounts). At the bottom of the list is the "Reset Device", which you need to click.

Before you, there will be another warning and the "Delete All" button. After clicking, the process of cleaning personal user data stored on the device will begin.

Confirmation of the general reset of Samsung smartphone data

If you use a graphic password, PIN or fingerprint sensor, or iris, you first need to unlock the option.

At the end of the process, the phone will reboot and appear before you in a pristinely pure form.

Despite its simplicity, this method has a significant drawback: to use it, it is necessary that the phone is loaded into the system.

Method 2: Factory Recovery

This hard-reset option is applicable when the device fails to boot the system, for example, during a cyclic reboot (boot loop).

Turn off the device. To enter the "Recovery Mode", simultaneously hold down the power button of the screen, "Volume Up" and "Home".

Sign in to the Samsung Smartphone Recovery

In case your device does not have the last key, just hold down the screen on plus "Volume Up".

When the standard screensaver with the words "Samsung Galaxy" appears on the display, release the power button and hold the rest for about 10 seconds. A recovery mode menu should appear.

Stock Recovery Menu in Samsung Smartphone

In case it didn't work, repeat points 1-2 again while holding the buttons a little longer.

When accessing Recovery, press the "Volume Down" button to select "Wipe data / factory reset". By selecting it, confirm the action by pressing the power button on the screen.

Resetting data in Samsung smartphone recovery

In the menu that appears, use "Volume Down" again to select

"Yes".

Confirmation item to delete all data in the Samsung recovery

Confirm the selection with the power button.

At the end of the cleaning process, you will be returned to the main menu. In it, select the option "Reboot system now".

Reboot after cleaning in Recovery in a Samsung smartphone

The device will reboot with already cleared data.

This system reset option will clear the memory, bypassing Android, allowing you to fix the above-mentioned boot loop. As in other ways, this action will delete all user data, so backup is desirable.

How to make shortcut "My Apps" from Google Play

There is no doubt that you are opening Google Play for one reason only: app updates. You also do this to install new programs, but mainly to update much more often. And in order to reduce the number of unnecessary clicks, and accordingly reduce the time to perform this task, there is one trick. On the desktop, you can place the shortcut "My Applications":

1. Place the Google Play app on your desktop.

2. Hold your finger on the application icon until the pop-up menu appears.

3. In the menu that appears, there will be only one line: "My Applications".

4. Hold your finger on this line and place a new icon in an empty

area of the desktop.

"About the application" through the multitasking menu

For each application under the Android operating system, there is a page "About the application". With it, you can remove the application, check the consumption of traffic, batteries, RAM, and clear the cache of the selected program, and much more. Users get on this page most often because the application is malfunctioning or has stopped running altogether. You can get to this page through the "Settings" menu item, but this is very long and tedious. For this there is one simple way that very few people know:

1. Open the multitasking menu on your device.

2. Find the application you need.

3. Hold your finger on the application icon (left side of the program).

4. After that, the icon in the form of the letter "i" will appear on the right side.

5. By clicking on this button you will be taken to the page "About the application".

Lock the desired application on the device display

A smartphone or tablet is your personal thing. It can store both personal photos and confidential documents. And here you are asked to "go to Facebook", "let me check email", etc. How to avoid being in this situation, with such information at risk? It is good that Google has also thought about this situation.

The Android operating system has a great feature called "In-app lock". Asked to check the mail? You can prevent people from being able to exit the Gmail application and see, for example, your photos. To do this, you need to activate this function:

1. Go to the menu item "Settings".

2. Next, select "Security" (in Android About, this item is called "Security and location).

3. Find the item "Pin application" in the list (in Android 8.0 - Lock in the application). Move the desired sliders to the active state.

After you activate this function and go to the multitasking menu, you will see that in the bottom right corner of each application there is a special icon in the form of a paper clip. By pressing it, the application is blocked on the device display.

"Quick Icons"

One of the best features of the Android operating system is the ability to customize the icons that are in the notification blind. In addition to a huge selection of standard icons, you can download others. For example:

1. Weather Tile - weather and Temperature

2. Quick Search Tile - quick access to online search

3. Tile - creating individual icons

To set up the number and icons you need:

1. Open the notification curtain.

2. Click on the pencil icon.

3. Arrange the icons to your liking or add new ones.

Traffic saving

Unfortunately, there are still people who think about the amount of traffic that a smartphone consumes. It is especially offensive when applications that run in the background "eat" your precious megabytes, and you do not even suspect it. Fortunately, Android has a great feature called Traffic Saving. With it, you can limit background data transfer for some applications.

1. Go to the menu item "Settings".

2. In the list, find the "Data transfer" item (in Android, O - Network, and Internet). Next, click on the item "Saving traffic" (in Android 8.0 - Data transfer - Saving traffic).

Select the applications that you want to restrict Internet access in the background.

Hiding notifications

Undoubtedly, if you are an advanced user of technology, then you probably have either a fingerprint or a pin code for unlocking your device. Nevertheless, what about the notifications that are visible on the lock screen? You can simply hide them, for this:

1. Open the "Settings" menu item.

2. Select "Notifications" (Security & Location - Blocked Screen Settings).

3. After that, select the form in which to display notifications; there will be several options: not to display notifications, to show notifications in full, or hide personal information).

Adding features to a fingerprint scanner

Today, many smartphones have a built-in fingerprint sensor (fingerprint scanner). In addition to its obvious function, it can also perform others. To do this, the Google Play app store has a great program called "Fingerprint Quick Action".

With the help of this program, you can select specific tasks for such actions as a single click on the scanner, a quick swipe, and double tap. I tried it personally, and it is a really handy thing.

Charging station

Galaxy can serve as a charging station for any other device. It can be either a smartphone or wireless headphones or a smartwatch. In addition, the S10 can simultaneously charge itself and charge the gadget lying on it.

Fast wireless charging

One of the main problems with wireless charging is the very slow process of replenishing battery capacity. If the full charge on the wire takes about an hour and a half, then on the Qi-platform this time will stretch to 2.5-3 hours.

Samsung solved this problem. The entire line of the Galaxy S10 supports fast wireless charging technology, which provides a two-fold increase in the power supply. The company said that the 3400 mAh battery in the Galaxy S10 will be charged at the Samsung branded station in just an hour and a half.

Instagram in the camera app

Samsung has entered into a large partnership with the social network and has added a special mode to the standard camera application for the Galaxy S10 smartphones. Using it, you can immediately take a snapshot to Instagram, without switching between applications.

In addition, Instagram mode can be selected as a tool for creating a panorama. After receiving the finished picture, users will be able to attach stickers to it directly in the camera application and select one of the available social network filters.

Cryptocurrency and security in your Galaxy

For the first time in the company's history, the Galaxy smartphone received protection at the hardware level for storing personal keys from cryptocurrency wallets and mobile services with blockchain support.

The option is implemented based on Samsung Knox, a proprietary mobile security solution pre-installed on most current Samsung devices. Knox on the Galaxy S10 for the first time received protection at the hardware level, which eliminates the possibility of hacking the system from the outside.

☐

Chapter 8 Apps and games

For your advanced device, there are many interesting games and applications. In this chapter, we will cover only some of them.

InstaMini

This is an instant camera in your smartphone. With this application, you get not only high-quality, but also instant snapshots with one click, and with a simple shaking of the phone, you can see how the image appears.

The main advantage of this application is its high resolution for snapshots. You can also add a location to the photo. There is a function of tracking people in the photo. It is very easy to manage and has a convenient and colorful interface.

RoboForm password manager

This is a password manager with form-filling function. With it you will get access to all your passwords from all your devices. And of course, the application provides secure login to the system (websites and applications) with the click of a button. It stores your passwords, auto-complete form, and supports all applications.

Just reminder with alarm

If you often forget about things, this app for you. A simple application that will remind you. This program just reminds you of something at some point. No more, no less. In this there are voice recognition functions, as well as full configuration of each reminder and backup and restore.

IF tracker

This application is for holding and monitoring your intermittent fasts. It tracks your progress during fasting and helps you maintain a healthy lifestyle. In this application, everything is explained quite simply and colorfully. Present functions: Visual presentation of posts, your progress, notifications, as well as backup

Monument browser

This is a fast, secure, and easy-to-use browser with a combination of beautiful design and unique exclusive features. It has a built-in ad blocker and a high-speed download manager. In addition, you can configure the application to erase all your data after the end of the session.

Glimpse notifications

This is a simple application for viewing notifications on the lock screen without pressing the power button. With this application, you can view notifications directly from the locked display, including nothing.

KWGT

This is an application that contains many possibilities for those who want to make their desktop unique. It has layouts and advanced settings for widget types such as world time, astronomical information, battery, memory status, weather, text widgets, maps, analog clock, and more. And all this can be customized.

Chat bin

This is a convenient and simple application for saving correspondence. With this application you can always read deleted messages or chats. In addition, it provides you with the opportunity to read the message without notifying the interlocutor.

With this you have access to the full chat history, hidden reading of messages, notifications, and sending messages without saving the number.

App Tiles

This is a very useful application to optimize the speed of launching applications. You can add up to 6 shortcuts for applications to your quick switch area in the notification panel. At the same time, this area is available in any application and at any time.

Prime weather

This is a very convenient and useful weather application for mobile devices. In fact, this is a simple application to view the weather in your city, but with an excellent widget and a great interface.

Opus player

This is an audio player that has a number of non-standard features. With it, you can even choose how to play audio files: the main speaker, voice speaker, or audio output. In addition, it provides many features for managing your audio messages, making it the best audio manager for WhatsApp voice memos.

Games

Before you play the game, set the resolution on your Galaxy S10.

Samsung Galaxy S10 supports various resolutions. In our review of the Samsung Galaxy S10, we noted that the phone has a native resolution of 1440 × 3040 pixels, out of the box it has been reduced to 1080 × 2280.

You can change this in the "Settings" menu using the slider to achieve the original resolution of 1440 × 3040, or reduce it to 720 × 1520 pixels. Low resolution makes the text uneven, and reduces the detail in the game, which makes it imperfect. Personally, we prefer the highest resolution or WQHD variant, as it is called.

Samsung Galaxy S10 Game Launcher and gaming tools explained

Samsung Galaxy S10 Game Launcher organizes all your games in one place, allowing you to customize them to your liking. This is useful for getting the most out of your games if you switch between multiple titles, letting you choose one of three settings for each of them. They speak for themselves. Focus on Energy Saving, Balanced, and Focus on Performance.

Going deeper, you will find the ability to set the frame rate (maximum 60 frames per second) and enable the so-called "Low Resolution" in the game, although it does not determine which resolution it is. Samsung warns that the individual game settings take precedence over general game performance settings and that changing the settings for each game can lead to incorrect game operation.

In addition, there are gaming tools that allow you to take screenshots, record video, decide whether you want to receive calls and notifications, or turn on Dolby Atmos for better sound quality. These features are easy to use, although we felt that the effects of Dolby Atmos are more pronounced when using headphones, such as the AKG pair, packed in the Galaxy S10 for immersive sound.

At first, we played PUBG Mobile. The default value is High, while

Ultra HD is currently unavailable. While the game can cover the entire screen, having a dual front camera breaks the dive, forcing us to play it with a black stripe along the top.

The gameplay of PUBG Mobile on the Samsung Galaxy S10 was smooth, with dense foliage, clear structures, and abundant weapons in native resolution WQHD. Whether it was lively shooting or running from intense bombardment, the PUBG Mobile frame rate was stable, with no slowdown or delay at all. Playing several rounds on the Erangel map, the Galaxy S10 allowed us to easily win chicken dinners. PUBG Mobile on the Samsung Galaxy S10 showed excellent performance, without the need for tuning on our part.

It was a similar scenario with Asphalt 9. Although the game did not start on the Samsung Galaxy S10 when launched via Google Play, now it does. There was no need to mess with the game to get the most out of it, by default using the highest settings and quality settings. Asphalt 9 was addicting on most phones at launch, which applies to the game on the Samsung Galaxy S10

Highly detailed car models with reflections, random details, such as water and dust, and breathtaking landscapes, such as the snow-capped peaks of the Himalayas and the rainy roads of Scotland. they all benefit from the higher resolution of the Galaxy S10 and the Infinity-O display, which makes the lighting and rain on Asphalt 9 look a little brighter than we used to see.

As for the competitor PUBG Mobile, Fortnite, the Galaxy S10 proved to be excellent, although this required a little modifying of the settings in the game. The game is set to Epic quality by default and is limited to a frame rate of 30 frames per second. Even though this is normal, it is interesting that the 3D resolution of the game is increased to 75%. This means that even if we played in the resolution of 1440 × 3040, choosing the resolution in the settings of the Galaxy S10, the game will still produce a resolution of 1080 × 2280.

Therefore, to get the most out of this, we had to set the 3D resolution slider in Fortnite to 100 percent. By sticking with the Epic preset and the 30 frames per second limit, you get smooth and stable gameplay.

The powerful internal components of the Galaxy S10 combined with the Infinity-O display do justice to the colorful locations, guns, and weapons of Fortnite, making them look even better.

If you want a smoother experience, you can choose the "High" setting for graphics quality, which allows you to set the frame rate to 60 frames per second, but it does not look so sharp. It still looks good, but for us, higher visual accuracy and a limited frame rate were simply better.

No matter what you choose, track down chests, explore forests, or just shoot enemies close to or from afar, it was great, and a step forward compared to Fortnite on Note 9. In fact, we would even say that the Samsung Galaxy S10 is probably the best mobile phone for Fortnite or others game available on Android at the moment.

Conclusion

The quality of communication for this smartphone is standard. There are no complaints. Ring volume is slightly increased compared with the previous generation, the speakers have become better. To say that S10 / S10+ is a revolution is impossible. It is an evolution, but with a very positive character. The new processor offers very good performance and updated cooling system, plus an adaptability of load settings, which translates into more time from one charge. Improved camera and additional modes are also a plus. The presence of a wide-angle camera is a huge, fat plus.

In these devices Samsung have added everything that is, in terms of technology, on the market. They have become the most charged. Of course, these models do not exist in a vacuum-free space, and Samsung set prices based on the iPhone, no doubt.

A comparison with both the iPhone XS / XS Max, and the Mate 20

Pro will be made. In my opinion, the S10 / S10+ definitely put Apple models on both blades. Those with a comparable cost lose almost everything. The Mate 20 Pro is not so bad. In short, we will meticulously compare and see which is better. In the meantime, we will leave it up to individual preferences.

Samsung produces great smartphones. Expensive ones. But there are not many alternatives for them, and most importantly, they evoke emotions. They need to be taken in hand to understand what is so good in them and why they are so cool. Go to the store and roll. These are the key products of 2019.

I hope, that you really enjoyed reading my book.

Thanks for buying the book anyway!